The Body

DATE DUE

Books by Tracy K. Smith

POETRY

The Body's Question
Duende
Life on Mars

MEMOIR

Ordinary Light

THE BODY'S QUESTION

Tracy K. Smith

Winner of the 2002 Cave Canem Poetry Prize

Selected and Introduced by Kevin Young

Graywolf Press

Publication of this volume is made possible in part by a grant provided by the Minnesota State Arts Board, through an appropriation by the Minnesota State Legislature; a grant from the Wells Fargo Foundation Minnesota; and a grant from the National Endowment for the Arts. Significant support has also been provided by the Bush Foundation; Target, Marshall Field's and Mervyn's with support from the Target Foundation; the McKnight Foundation; and other generous contributions from foundations, corporations, and individuals. To these organizations and individuals we offer our heartfelt thanks.

NATIONAL ENDOWMENT FOR THE ARTS

MINNESOTA STATE ARTS BOARD

Special funding for this title has been provided by the Jerome Foundation.

Published by Graywolf Press
250 Third Avenue North, Suite 600
Minneapolis, Minnesota 55401
All rights reserved.

www.graywolfpress.org

Published in the United States of America

ISBN 978-1-55597-391-9

6 8 10 12 13 11 9 7

Library of Congress Control Number: 2003101170

Cover art: Igor Solís, *Nacer* (detail)

Cover design: Christa Schoenbrodt, Studio Haus

Acknowledgments

Grateful acknowledgment is made to the editors of the following journals, in which versions of these poems originally appeared:

Arcade: "Joy" section II. (under the title "Not of the Dead but the Living")

Callaloo: "Joy" section IV. (under the title "Grammar"), "Five Dreams of Offspring," "Night Letters," "Wintering"

Post Road: "Self-Portrait As the Letter Y," "A Hunger So Honed"

"Drought" was featured on the Cave Canem web site (www.cavecanempoets.org).

"Studio," "The Machinery of Evening," "Dominion over the Beasts of the Earth," "What Fear Is," "Credulity," "Betty Blue," "Serenade," "Thirst," and "Something Like Dying, Maybe" were featured in the online magazine, *Muse Apprentice Guild* (www.muse-apprentice-guild.com).

"Bright" was broadcast on WNYE (91.5 FM, New York City).

for all my families

Contents

III.

IV.

Introduction by Kevin Young

Tracy Smith speaks many different languages. Besides the Spanish that graces the "Gospels" of her book's opening section, Smith also seems perfectly at home speaking of grief and loss, of lust and hunger, of joy and desire—which here often means the desire for desire, and a desire for language itself. As she puts it in "Mangoes": "Desire is a city of yellow houses / As it surrenders its drunks to the night." She also seems perfectly, intuitively aware that the root of the word *language* is "tongue"; indeed, in her best poems Smith seems to speak in tongues, to speak about that thing even beyond language, answering *The Body's Question* of her title.

And as that title implies, Smith speaks a body language. Appetite is a term that runs throughout the poems, both in title and theme—besides "Mangoes," the book's second section also speaks of "A Hunger So Honed" and "Appetite" itself. In section four the lively "Self-Portrait As the Letter Y" declares:

> You are pure appetite. I am pure
> Appetite. You are a phantom
> In that far-off city where daylight
> Climbs cathedral walls, stone by stolen stone.
> I am invisible here, like I like it.
> The language you taught me rolls
> From your mouth into mine
> The way kids will pass smoke
> Between them.

The appetite here is for language, one shared like smoke. The speaker's contentment with invisibility might seem like a relief after a half-century of invisibility as merely a negative metaphor for African American existence. Here, invisibility seems only one part of being, of blackness and desire in a universe bigger than we are.

Besides hunger, there's a thirst here, as in "Drought" where we see fully the California backdrop that grounds, as it were, these poems as no mere flights of fancy:

> And the brambles whispered.
> And my hands in their mischief.
>
> A spasm, a spark, a sweet murmuring flame
> That swallowed the creek-bed and spread,
> Mimicking water. A gorgeous traffic
> Flickering with light, as God is light.
> I led my shadow there and laid it down.
> And my shadow rose and entered me.
> And on the third day, it began to speak,
> Naming me.

The body here is holy, as is its shadow—Smith doesn't divide the two as some (or Western culture) might; instead, she sees the dark and light together. Her language here is almost biblical, yet full of that elusive thing good hip-hop emcee's have, *flow,* her lines themselves a "gorgeous traffic" that "mimics water."

My only question in reading this collection among the many submitted for this year's fourth annual Cave Canem Poetry Prize was: who was this being named? And naming such beauty, so boldly? What other emerging poet can you think of brave enough to name a poem, and indeed entire section of a collection, "Joy"? Much less have that "Joy" be an elegy where questioning the body means the body itself becomes a question? The poems seemed to come out of nowhere, like a powerful voice you might not expect from a slight frame; there was no hint of divadom, or trendiness; indeed, I wasn't sure how old or how young, even how male or female the singer was. For if the poems here are sure of anything, they are sure enough not to worry overmuch about who's talking when—we are, for all their sensual beauty, in the presence of poems unafraid to be without a body, all language and light. So reading the poems, submitted anonymously, gave no clue, at least to this reader, as to whose autobiography was behind them—a good thing in this case, as reading them we are left instead with a map of a million interiors that only hint at the mapmaker's hand.

Imagine my surprise then, after selecting the book, I found out I had known the author once upon a time! We both were early members of the Dark Room Collective, a group of black writers based in Boston, though at the time she was most active, I myself was out West writing—on a fellowship she would, as fate had it, hold a few years after—and I rarely if ever saw her work. I have a hunch even if I had, I couldn't have predicted the journey Smith's work would take in and between these poems, which seem unafraid to embrace all the many cultures that make up America, and specifically, that define the breadth of African American exprience. In this, Smith is welcome to the tradition as Jay Wright, and like Wright, evokes a point of view that sees the American West not as in a movie, but as a shared culture that the black cowboy and -girl proved a vital part of in history, if not image.

As a result, her poems seem to me concerned with place in the best sense. Though one poem announces a "Brief Touristic Account," Smith actually avoids the kind of emotional tourism often found in the poetry of the 1980s and 1990s, in part exactly by realizing her own stance, and also by recognizing that the only thing foreign might be the speaker of the poems. Smith knows places are strange only to the stranger. Take the "Account," which not only isn't touristic but also isn't exactly brief; the poem ends with a dream of water and the lines:

> By the time I lay down,
> Lying beside you was like
> Dangling a leg
>
> Over the edge
> Of a drifting boat.

The distance (and journey) such lines invoke could apply to what I gather is a lover who is at times elusive—but could as easily be talking about the book's relation to place (or desire or hunger) as something always nearby but always out of reach.

This seems Smith's view of language itself, which her poems struggle with and toward. She is unafraid of beauty, or of ugly, and in this alone would make Langston Hughes proud. But she also seems at home being down home as more obviously poetic—after all, the speaker is up late in "Self-Portrait" talking trash.

"Night" here, as in Hughes, is also a place—one of blackness triumphant and not merely mysterious (as it sometimes is in Wallace Stevens, a spirit here that guides but does not dominate, as in the very title "Self-Portrait As the Letter Y"). In "Night Letters" there is again loss, and desire, and hunger revealed at last to be "part anger"; what's more, there is the dark that, as she reminds us, is always with us: "Somewhere it is always night on the planet." But as with Hughes night is tender, and reassuring:

> I listen, knowing
> You are so far away I must be
> Inside you, knowing the night is a great,
> Soft, whispering, steady thing
> Going on in and around you
> And that I am in it.

Such reassurance carries through into the book's very structure, starting with a kind of benediction in "Something Like Dying, Maybe" and fittingly ending with "Prayer." I could quote the entire poem, indeed the entire book, as a sign of its unique ability to make departure a rehearsal, make a poem that is about both yearning and its realization—but it's enough to say Smith turns prayer to a thing made, into noun-ness, into "the Yes that is a lie / And the Yes that is not a lie." And into something redeeming for all of us.

As her very name announces, Smith is a maker, a wordsmith of the first order, and I welcome her work into the world.

The Body's Question

Something Like Dying, Maybe

Last night, it was bright afternoon
Where I wandered. Pale faces all around me.
I walked and walked looking for a door,
For some cast-off garment, looking for myself
In the blank windows and the pale blank faces.

I found my wristwatch from ten years ago
And felt glad awhile.
When it didn't matter anymore being lost,
The sky clouded over and the pavement went white.
I stared at my hands. Like new leaves,
Light breaking through from behind.

Then I felt your steady breathing beside me
And the mess of blankets where we slept.
I woke, touching ground gently
Like a parachutist tangled in low branches.
All those buildings, those marvelous bodies
Pulled away as though they'd never known me.

I.

Serenade

I am dancing with Luis,
The dancing *puto,*
Delirious with Spanish and moonlight,
With the scrawl of streets that led us here
To night in a foreign language.
We are dancing the *merengue*
And my body rings
With the ringing that wants to be answered.
As though I am a little drunk in the bones.
As though all along, my body has been waiting
To show me these trees, these nocturnal birds.

City of Restless Vendors, of Steep Embankments,
Of Padlocks and Bad Plumbing:
You have carried on this whole night
In the clatter of footsteps, in the private cadence of voices
And the silhouettes from which the voices spring.
You have carried on as two girls in a doorway,
As a figure the pretty one describes so vividly
It seems to hover in the air before them.
As the smoke trailing the gestures of certain men,
And the tobacco each removes from his teeth.

Luis takes my hand in his hand
And draws circles in the air
Above my head. I am spinning.
Sloppily at first, until my mind
Begins to understand that grace
Is a different phenomenon here,
And lets go of my two legs,
Allowing them to dance on their own
Like the legs of a chicken

Whose head dangles
A limp carnation
From its neck. I am spinning
So giddily the bottles of beer and liquor
And the bags bereft of their ice
Form one great lake of ecstatic liquid.
I want to race out now into the dark
That cradles us. Past the red
Tips of dragged-on cigarettes,
Past the tall weeds a few men
Wade out into, and the singing that reaches us
From the other side of the patio walls.

Earlier tonight in the plaza
Fireworks so close overhead
We might have touched them
On their way back down. People
Ate cotton candy and roast corn
Singing *No vale nada la vida*
　　　　La vida no vale nada,
Faces painted to resemble *calaveras.*
Is Luis crying? No—but makeup
Streaks his face like newsprint
That's been rained on.
I closed my eyes a moment ago.
Now daylight appears just about to rise
To its feet, like a guest
Who's sat all night
Keeping time to lively music.

Thirst

The old man they called Bagre
Who welcomed us with food
And rice-paper cigarettes
At the table outside his cabin
Was the one who told the soldiers
To sit down. They were drunk.
They'd seen the plates on our car
From the road and came to where
You and I and Bagre and his son
Sat laughing. I must have been
Drunk myself to laugh so hard
At what I didn't understand.

It was night by then. We smoked
To keep off the mosquitoes.
There was fish to eat—nothing but fish
Bagre and the other men caught.
The two little girls I'd played with
Were asleep in their hammocks.
Even Genny and Manuel,
Who rode with us and waited
While we hurried out of our clothes
And into those waves the color
Of atmosphere.

Before the soldiers sat down,
They stood there, chests ballooned.
When we showed them our papers,
They wanted something else.
One of them touched the back of my leg.
With your eyes, you told me
To come beside you. There were guns

Slung over their shoulders
Like tall sticks. They stroked them
Absently with their fingers.

Their leader was called Jorge.
I addressed him in the familiar.
I gave him a half-empty bottle
Of what we were drinking.
When it was empty, I offered to fill it
With water from the cooler.
He took a sip, spat it out
And called you by your name.
I didn't want to see you
Climb onto that jeep of theirs—so tall
And broad it seemed they'd ridden in
On elephants yoked shoulder to shoulder,
Flank to flank.

Maybe this is a story
About the old man they called Bagre.
The one with the crooked legs
That refused to run.
Maybe this is a story about being too old
To be afraid, and too young not to fear
Authority, and abuse it, and call it
By its name, and call it a liar.
Or maybe it's a story about the fish.
The ones hanging on branches

To dry, and the ones swimming
With eyes that would not shut
In water that entered them
And became them
And kept them from thirst.

Niña Fantasma

When he comes, Mario asks
Oiste la lluvia? and it sounds so perfect
I ask him to say it again. *Oiste la lluvia?*
For rain so sudden it is love,
Hunger in a foreign language.
Rain that bathed the mangroves,
Coconut orchard, the clay earth
Where Mario lay his Reina Isabel
Blessed ghost child
When her body let go its frail soul.

Mario sweeps up the leaves
Fallen during the night,
And his broom sighs *Isabel*
Across the ground. For cervine beauty.
For her footsteps in dust. For Irma,
Her mother, who wept into the salt air
When they found her Reinita
Her tiny queen recumbent
In a nest of vines. The child did not move,
Nor bother with the gnats that swarmed her.

Mario sweeps and his body remembers
Lifting her from the thicket, hugging
Her chill limbs to warm them
As he carried her the pathless mile home.
He followed where her fawn's legs pointed,
As though what lived in them was memory,
As though what coursed in them coursed
Toward the narrow bed
Where he would lay her down
And pull the leaves from her hair.

Brief Touristic Account

III.13

It was evening. You were waiting
With a friend, lights flickering—
Kerosene
And the embers
Of nervous cigarettes.

The driver had slowed
To mouth the number of each house
We drove past before yours. Yours—
Lamp-lit and silent, though in the silence
Just after knocking, I heard

A faint music and your voice
Interrupting itself
To reply.

III.14

There was light entering through doorways,
And the furrows of sheet we rose from.

There was the traffic outdoors,
And the traffic of shadows indoors.

There were the wet prints
Where our feet had been,

And the two towels
Drying in the sun.

III.17

The patio door
Framed a tree-occluded sky,
First pale, then red, then dark,
Then darker. Each man
Who went outside came back
Buoyant, like one about
To deliver a punchline.

Sometimes I rose
At the same time as one
Of them, and I'd follow him
Or he'd follow me over
The tangle of legs and bottles
Spoking out from the table
We sat circling. Then I'd

Go in the door on the right
To piss quietly, thinking
What it must be like
To stand alone in the garden
Sending great, glad,
Shimmering arcs
Out into the night.

III.22

You, her, him, me.
Four figures in two languages,
The beginning of a riddle
The moon didn't ponder,

Squinting down
From beside the one star
That almost lit our way.

III.24

The worm in the bottle
Was supposed to suggest
What exactly?
Its last happy exhalations,
Lungs giddy, mouth spilling
A necklace of miniscule bubbles
Through a world suddenly liquid,
Suddenly amber with a warmth
That scalded the eyes—
Which blinked once, sealing shut—
Then traveled the slender nerves
Along its body to the nerve knot
Whose final message
Was to curl around itself
Like a boutonniere
Before going limp?

Or something slower?
The long fall, the gradual
Unblurring. Disbelief
And then relief.
As when I woke
To the crackling of logs,
You in the foreground
Prodding the flames?

III.26

You woke when the moon dropped below the black waves,
Our tent, shone-through by pinpricks of light,

Giving the sense of a sky
Under the sky.
And we had the same idea:
Remove the tent roof,
Draw them closer,
Offer that bright heaven

The glimpse of its inverse:
Uncelestial simplicity,

Finitude. And as synonym for
Love, both noun and verb:
Our bodies, weighted, lightless,
Recumbent.

III.28

There was the room devoid of light.
The room so dark it disappeared
From around us,
The dark a tall space
Around the shallow space
Our breathing filled.

There were the neighbors' voices
Singing to God, and the delicate

Violence of our bodies renouncing speech,
Heat making the room still,
Amplifying each sound.

III.30

We slept
A few hours only
In the small bed
In your mother's house.
She slept
The same few hours
Behind a curtain
That split the room in two.

You were the first
To disappear,
Eyes dreaming,
Lungs letting go their
Deep unconscious sighs,
So effortlessly rhythmic
You must have dreamt

Water—current
Spilling into chill current
Like dark muscles
Veined with white—
Already so far gone
By the time I lay down,

Lying beside you was like
Dangling a leg

Over the edge
Of a drifting boat.

Gospel: Manuel

There's a story told here
By those of us who daydream
To the music of crystal and steel.

We brought it down
From mountains built of fog
Where we left the girls we married

And old men married to the earth.
We fed on it when there was nothing.
From hunger, it grew large.

And from that dark spot low in each of us
Where alone we disappear to, breathing
The cool nothing of night, letting the city

Farther inside with each siren bleat
Each assault of neon light, grounding
Ourselves to this world with one hand

Under the head, the other invisible—
From that spot it became a woman.
Part mother, part more.

We learned it by heart
So that each time one of us told it,
He told it tasting smoke and corn

And the red earth dug up
By gangs of faithless dogs.
He told it in barely a voice at all,

Almost not wanting to believe.

Gospel: Miguel (el Lobito)

My brother shook me awake
And handed me our father's
Hunting gun. I followed him

To the hill that sits between towns.
Below: all of ours
And all of theirs, racing around

like two teams
After a leather ball.
It was a war, he told me.

Whoever won
Would go into the woods
And take whatever grew.

That night, we sat on the hill
Watching the fires burn.
They'll still be slaves,

He said. Nothing
That means anything
Has changed.

Gospel: Luis

The river we crossed to get here
Is a wide, black, furious serpent
That swells with laughter
When you step close.

At its tail, in a snarl
Of branches where the rocks
Come up high enough and land
Stalls the current,

That's where they say you'll find
Bundles of money
And, more than anything, bodies
Of horses and boys like us.

I remember how deep
The dark got.

Nothing we could do but wait.
Even the sound
Of my own voice in my head
Echoed, got lost

In the sound of what roamed,
Eyes lit like sparks
A house gives off when it burns.
I tried to dream of what animal

Would shine like that from far away.

Gospel: Juan

We crossed the border
Hours before dawn
Through a hole
Dug under a fence.

We crossed
Dressed as soldiers,
Faces painted
Mud green.

The *coyotes*
That promised
We'd make it, gave us
A straw broom

To drag behind,
Erasing our tracks.
They gave us meat
Drugged for the dogs.

Farther off,
There were engines,
Voices, a light
That swept the ground.

We crossed
On our bellies.
I wonder
If we'll ever stand up.

Gospel: Alejandro (el Monstruo)

And then it was day and we were free,
Riding in the back of an enormous truck,
Laughing, peeing over the side.

When I saw the hills, how they resembled
The bodies of our women, I knew this country
Never stopped being our country.

But there are people who don't know
And will never care. White faces,
Black faces that move past us

Like empty plates.
That's what they think of us.
I work and work. At night

I climb to the sixth floor
Carrying bags of beer. I sit up
With whoever's awake and before long

We're floating. *Embriagados.*
Happy as we've ever been. Half listening
To the music, the voices outside.

Sometimes, we make ourselves believe
We never left, the traffic
Nothing but wind against the roof.

Gospel: Jesús

I'd like to smash a goblet in my fist.
Instead, I watch my hands baptize each piece,
making piles of the things I have watched myself
make new.
                I watch my hands
until I am watching out from my hands—
now in air, now water, each element
a shadow of the other.

II.

Drought

1.

The hydrangea begins as a small, bright world.
Mother buries rusty nails, and the flowers
Weep blue and pink. I am alone in the garden,
And like all else that is living, I lean into the sun.

Each bouquet will cringe and die in time
While the dry earth watches. It is ugly,
And the earth is ugly to allow it. Still, the petals
Curl and drop. Mother calls it an exquisite waste,

But there is no choice. I learn how:
Before letting go, open yourself completely.
Wait. When the heavens fail to answer,
Curse the heavens. Wither and bend.

2.

We go to the lake. I am the middle son
And most beautiful, my face and chest,
All of me, brown with sun. I ride to the lake
With my brothers and sister, and the smells
Of asphalt and dirt fill me with happy rage.
I am twelve, and the voices I carry know how to obey.
When the blades of grass catch my spokes,
There is a quick *twit* when the blades snap.

The others giggle near shore but I am swimming
Toward the island in the center, a vacant country.
The black water bids me farther.
Out past the people speckling the lake
To the cold, cold center and that island's empty shore.
The syllables of my name skip across like smooth stone,
And when they reach me, my lungs shrink to fists.
I flail upright and the waves lash out in my wake.

3.

Not the flame, but what it promised.
Surrender. To be quenched of danger.
I torched toothpicks to watch them
Curl around themselves like living things,
Panicked and aglow. I would wake,
Sheets wrinkled and damp, and rise
From that print of myself,
That sleep-slack dummy self.
Make me light.

No one missed my shadow
Moving behind the house, so I led it
To the dry creek-bed and laid it down
Among thistledown, nettle,
Things that hate water as I hate
That weak, ash-dark self.
I stood above it,
A silent wicked thing that would not beg.
I crouched, and it curled before me.
I rose, and it stretched itself, toying.

And the brambles whispered.
And my hands in their mischief.

A spasm, a spark, a sweet murmuring flame
That swallowed the creek-bed and spread,
Mimicking water. A gorgeous traffic

Flickering with light, as God is light.
I led my shadow there and laid it down.
And my shadow rose and entered me.
And on the third day, it began to speak,
Naming me.

Betty Blue

I have always been this beautiful
And this dead.

Like pages ripped from a passionate book,
I have always been stitched

To the inside of someone's greatcoat,
Someone's tender cheek.

From my soft cot, I look only up,
Never out, glad

For the implacable pale blue of this room
Where I'm bundled and belted down,

Waiting for something that happened long ago—
Before medicine, before intermission,

Before that warm weight above me or below,
Breathing and saying my name.

The shapes of words enter and play
At making sense. A globe

Of daylight, like a cat, caught
In tree boughs.

I wanted a different kind of pain. For it to come
From inside and want out

And to rip its way there, howling that fat, flat way
Life does.

To lift up my skirt and forget for once
What to expect.

Mangoes

The woman in a blouse
The color of daylight
Motions to her daughter not to slouch.
They wait without luggage.
They have been waiting
Since before the station smelled
Of cigarettes. Shadows
Fill the doorway and fade
One by one
Into bloated faces.
She'd like to swat at them
Like the lazy flies
That swarm her kitchen.

She considers her hands, at rest
Like pale fruits in her lap. Should she
Gather them in her skirt and hurry
Down the tree in reverse, greedy
For a vivid mouthful of something
Sweet? The sun gets brighter
As it drops low. Soon the room
Will glow gold with late afternoon.
Still no husband, face creased from sleep,
His one bag across his chest. Soon
The windows will grow black. Still
No one with his hand always returning
To the hollow below her back.

Desire is a city of yellow houses
As it surrenders its drunks to the night.
It is the drunks on ancient bicycles
Warbling into motionless air,

And the pigeons, asleep in branches,
That will repeat the same songs tomorrow
Believing them new. Desire is the woman
Awake now over a bowl of ashes
That flutter and drop like abandoned feathers.
It's the word *widow* spelled slowly in air
With a cigarette that burns
On its own going.

Appetite

It's easy to understand that girl's father
Telling her it's time to come in and eat.
Because the food is good and hot.
Because he has worked all day
In the same shirt, unbuttoned now
With its dirty neck and a patch
With his name on the chest.

The girl is not hungry enough
To go in. She has spent all day
Indoors playing on rugs, making her eyes
See rooms and houses where there is only
Shadow and light. She knows
That she knows nothing of the world,
Which makes the stoop where she kneels
So difficult to rise from.

But her father is ready to stuff himself
On mashed potatoes and sliced bread,
Ready to raise a leg of chicken to his lips,
Then a wing; to feel the heat enter through his teeth,
Skin giving way like nothing else
Will give way to him in this lifetime.

He's ready to take a bite
Of the pink tomatoes while his mouth
Is still full with something else,
To hurry it down his throat
With a swig of beer, shrugging
When his wife says, *You're setting*
A bad example. It doesn't matter—

Too many eyes without centers
For one day. Too many
Dice, cards, dogs with faces like sharks
Tethered to chains. It gives him
An empty feeling below his stomach,
And all he can think to call it
Is appetite. And so he will lie
When he kisses his napkin and says
Hits the spot, as his daughter will lie
When she learns to parrot him,
Not yet knowing what her own appetite
Points to.

A Hunger So Honed

Driving home late through town
He woke me for a deer in the road,
The light smudge of it fragile in the distance,

Free in a way that made me ashamed for our flesh—
His hand on my hand, even the weight
Of our voices not speaking.

I watched a long time
And a long time after we were too far to see,
Told myself I still saw it nosing the shrubs,

All phantom and shadow, so silent
It must have seemed I hadn't wakened,
But passed into a deeper, more cogent state—

The mind a dark city, a disappearing,
A handkerchief
Swallowed by a fist.

I thought of the animal's mouth
And the hunger entrusted it. A hunger
So honed the green leaves merely maintain it.

We want so much,
When perhaps we live best
In the spaces between loves,

That unconscious roving,
The heart its own rough animal.
Unfettered.

        The second time,
There were two that faced us a moment
The way deer will in their Greek perfection,

As though we were just some offering
The night had delivered.
They disappeared between two houses,

And we drove on, our own limbs,
Our need for one another
Greedy, weak.

Credulity

We believe we are giving ourselves away,
And so it feels good,
Our bodies swimming together
In afternoon light, the music
That enters our window as far
From the voices that made it
As our own minds are from reason.

There are whole doctrines on loving.
A science. I would like to know everything
About convincing love to give me
What it does not possess to give. And then
I would like to know how to live with nothing.
Not memory. Nor the taste of the words
I have willed you whisper into my mouth.

Five Dreams of Offspring

You are bathing the baby
In a tin basin used
For boiling hominy.
You dip a cup
Beneath the surface
And tip it
Over the baby's head,
Tracing the curve
From crown to nape
With your thumb.
And again, this time tracing
The ears. Papery things,
Each with its crescent-shaped
Nimbus of down.

Brown leaves
Cough at your feet
As if to ask, *What business*
Is this of yours? As if
To keep you from knowing
To lift the baby from the water
And hold her so she believes
She has taken flight.
The brown leaves want
To wake you, but first
They want to call your attention
To the heap they have formed
Where you stand,
Each dark shape a waiting hand.

• • •

She will dry quickly in the sun.
She will cry for shade,
And when you shade her,
Watching her eyelids lower,
Leaning into her slight heft
That rests easily
Against your chest,
You will scan the yard
For answers—a mound of leaves
Like earth atop a fresh grave—
To the question that quickens
Your shallow breaths.

      • • •

In a tin basin
Used for boiling hominy,
You are bathing the baby,

Brown leaves
At your feet. She blinks
When flying shadows cross.

Outside of words,
She thinks you and she
Are birds

Like all the others,
Your wings and her tufts
Bobbing in and out of water,

Splashing beads of light
That drop back into the basin
After brief flight.

• • •

Wind would sweep the sky
Of its faint clouds, thin
As soap that has been handled
To a papery thinness.

And it would trouble the leaves
That, motionless, seem
Not just to watch, but to hover
On the verge of speaking.

• • •

You are bathing the baby.
Brown leaves cough at your feet.
Papery things
Like the bodies
Of crabs that have dried
On the beach, which
Is where you take the baby
Certain by now she is yours,
Born of your waking fear,
Your slow waiting.

Wintering

A white day breaks through the dusky cloud
That was last night, when you lifted me
Onto the pillows and whispered marvelous things
Into my thighs. I don't want to rise
From this bed or this life, your head heavy
Beside mine in the low space
Where everything that means something happens.

That first night, there was tinny music
Coming from the kitchen, and men
Masquerading as monks. You appeared
In the dark, two red horns among
Ink-colored curls. We shared a cup of rum.
Your mouth burned like a drunk's
When you touched it to mine.

You led me down the narrow streets of that city.
Stone pavements. Iron gratings.
Geraniums. It was autumn.
People celebrated the return of their dead.
At the time I did not say, *Please, God, let me*
Know nothing else ever but this. I watched
For spaces between stones where I might trip.

White light bears down on the wordless sky.
I dreamt again of my mother.
I sat beside her, trying to forget the years of grief,
Trying to understand the puzzle of life in her body.
I speak another language, I told her. *I love.*
She watched without speaking, as if to say
Think of where I have been, what I've seen.

III.

Joy

In memoriam KMS 1936–1994

Imagining yourself a girl again,
You ask me to prepare a simple meal
Of dumplings and kale.

The body is memory.
You are nine years old,
Playing hospital with your sisters.

These will be my medicine,
You tell them, taking a handful
Of the raisins that you love.

They've made the room dark
And covered you with a quilt,
Though this is the South in summer.

The body is appetite.
You savor the kale,
Trusting this one need.

But the body is cautious,
Does not want more
Than it wants. Soon

There will be a traffic
Of transparent tubes, striking
Their compromise with the body.

When you close your eyes,
I know you are listening
To a dark chamber

Around a chord of light.
I know you are deciding
That the body's a question:

What do you believe in?

It will rain tomorrow, as it rained in the days after you died.
And I will struggle with what to wear, and take a place on the bus
Among those I will only ever know by the shape their shoulders make
Above the backs of the seats before mine. It is November,

And storm clouds ascend above the roofs outside my window.
I don't know anymore where you've gone to. Whether your soul
Waits here—in my room, in the kitchen with the newly blown bulb—
Or whether it rose instantly to the kingdom of hosannas. Some nights,

Walking up my steps in the dark, digging for the mail and my keys,
I know you are far, infinitely far from us. That you watch
In the way one of us might pause a moment to watch a frenzy of ants,
Wanting to help, to pick up the crumb and put it down
Close to their hill, seeing their purpose that clearly.

Days like this, when I don't know
Whether it's worse being weighed down
By an umbrella I'm bound to lose, I wish
I could pick up the phone
And catch your voice on the other end
Telling me how to bake a salmon
Or get the stains out of my white clothes.

I wish I could stand at my window
Watching those other dark bodies
Moving back and forth through kitchens
Or climbing stairs, heavy
With the heaviness of the everyday,
And hear that long-distance phonograph silence
Between words like *salt* and *soak*. Sometimes

The phone will ring late at night
And I'll think about answering
With a question: *What's the recipe*
For lasagna? Sometimes the smoke
Off my own cigarette fools me, and I think
It's you running your hands
Along the dust-covered edges of things.

These logs, hacked so sloppily
Their blonde grains resemble overdone poultry,
Are too thick to catch.

I crumple paper to encourage the flame,
And for a brief moment everything is lit.

But the logs haven't caught,
Just seem to smolder and shrink
As the heat works its way to their center.

Getting to what I want
Will be slow going and mostly smoke.

Years ago during a storm,
I knelt before the open side
Of a blue and white miniature house,

Moving the dolls from room to room
While you added kindling to the fire.

It is true that death resists the present tense.
But memory does death one better. Ignores the future.
We sat in that room until the wood was spent.

We never left the room.
The wood was never spent.

IV.

Self-Portrait As the Letter Y

1.

I waved a gun last night
In a city like some ancient Los Angeles.
It was dusk. There were two girls
I wanted to make apologize,
But the gun was useless.
They looked sideways at each other
And tried to flatter me. I was angry.
I wanted to cry. I wanted to bury the pistol,
But I would've had to walk miles.
I would've had to learn to run.

2.

I have finally become that girl
In the photo you keep among your things,
Steadying myself at the prow of a small boat.
It is always summer here, and I am
Always staring into the lens of your camera,
Which has not yet been stolen. Always
With this same expression. Meaning
I see your eye behind the camera's eye.
Meaning that in the time it takes
For the tiny guillotine
To open and fall shut, I will have decided
I am just about ready to love you.

3.

Sun cuts sharp angles
Across the airshaft adjacent.

They kiss. They kiss again.
Faint clouds pass, disband.

Someone left a mirror
At the foot of the fire escape.

They look down. They kiss.

She will never be free
Because she is afraid. He

Will never be free
Because he has always

Been free.

4.

Was kind of a rebel then.
Took two cars. Took
Bad advice. Watched people's
Asses. Sniffed their heads.

Just left, so it looked
Like those half-sad cookouts,
Meats never meant to be
Flayed, meant nothing.

Made promises. Kept going.
Prayed for signs. Stooped
For coins. Needed them.
Had two definitions of family.

Had two families. Snooped.
Forgot easily. Well, didn't
Forget, but knew when it was safe
To remember. Woke some nights

Against a wet pillow, other nights
With the lights on, whispering
The truest things
Into the receiver.

5.

A dog scuttles past, like a wig
Drawn by an invisible cord. It is spring.
The pirates out selling fakes are finally
Able to draw a crowd. College girls
Show bare skin in good faith. They crouch
Over heaps of bright purses, smiling,
Willing to pay. Their arms
Swing forward as they walk away, balancing
That new weight on naked shoulders.
The pirates smile, too, watching
Pair after pair of thighs carved in shadow
As girl after girl glides into the sun.

6.

You are pure appetite. I am pure
Appetite. You are a phantom
In that far-off city where daylight
Climbs cathedral walls, stone by stolen stone.
I am invisible here, like I like it.

The language you taught me rolls
From your mouth into mine
The way kids will pass smoke
Between them. You feed it to me
Until my heart grows fat. I feed you
Tiny black eggs. I feed you
My very own soft truth. We believe.
We stay up talking all kinds of shit.

Fire Escape Fantasy

This is a city of tunnels and great heights,
Fierce tracks where you find yourself
Just going, face fixed, body braced
Against questions, against knowing,
The lights below and out across proof
Of the thin liquid we float in.

Windows open to the faint breath
Of the inevitable, I pray
To my god of smoke, of science,
Of the people I despise. I draw
The strings of my life tighter,
Feeling nothing. There are small men

Whose small fists rattle, spilling dice
Onto the pavement like teeth, so that our night
Is a kind of agitated music. That's why women
Wear worry and cover their heads, let their words
Drop like shot birds from the higher windows.
Every night here one of us is sliced open.

A woman lifts her arm and brings it down.
Or a cop. This is obviously a question.
The child that cries out from below
Repeats the answer again and again: obedience.
This century was not designed to be felt. Still, I test
Like a girl determined to break herself apart.

Success must hurt. Must yield sharp evidence.
I'll have to lie to get to it.
                              Like love.

Night Letters

TUESDAY

Each night, a small cat steps closer
To my window. Braver and braver.
Soon there will be tracks like dusky clovers

Across the covers, and straight hairs
On your empty side of the bed. I make a
Coaxing sound with my lips,

Hold out two fingers to the night
Thinking to lure it that way.
Sometimes, the nights are so silent

I forget why I'm here.
Your belongings ignore me, go on
With their wordless conversation,

Confident you'll return soon
To rub your hands along their lines,
Erasing distance. Sometimes,

I want to do what I did once
In a frightening dream. Take a cab
Up past where the avenues arc down

And streetlamps converge and disappear,
Then step out and take a look
At whom I'm with. In the dream,

I didn't want to but I did, forced
By pointless evenings just like these,
The bed grinning up from the floor.

Sleep, it seems to say. But I don't sleep.

In the dream, the face beside me
Was blotched and wet,
And the strong hand clamped my arm.

Why do dreams betray us?
My limbs were too heavy, steps
Dazed, dizzy, going wherever.

I remember those mute, reluctant blocks
That led to the dark room
Where my mind struggled to wake.

Remember my own bright shirt
Like a defeated flag
Among the heap of clothes.

Why does it take you so long
To come for me?

FRIDAY

Curtains flayed, days glide by
Like southward birds. I am alone,
Living like a child in a deserted house.
Some days I am glad.
Others, a hunger

That is part anger
Makes me vivid. I am growing
With a little of you inside me,
Forgetting so many things.
All the words for reason
Lie heaped at the back of a closet
I will not open
Until the sun has crossed my window
For the last time without waking you.
The 13th again.
Unseasonably cold.

SUNDAY

Sometimes, all I wish for
Are those exhausted nights in San Francisco
Before you were real. When I'd finish
A party and change slowly into my clothes,
Then go for a drink with Robert
Or Michael at a place where women
Weren't supposed to matter.
I was anyone I wanted to be. Lola.
Laura. I could talk and talk
And my legs never stopped moving.

WEDNESDAY

A man who looks like an ancient
Version of your father
Buries his hand in a bag of crumbs.
Pigeons rush his ankles,
Whispering in the voice of the sea.

I'm tired. I've forgotten what's important.
Maybe I ought to go back to my room
And turn on the stereo, follow my thoughts
To that place in the middle where they just . . . .

Somewhere it is always night on the planet.

SATURDAY

Me with my feet wet
From the sky that shattered
Like an angry miracle.
Me perched every wet night
On the edge of that sleep
Where you come to me.
Where you step forward on dark gravel
And we begin.

Outside, buses cruise past
Like ancient, leaf-eating beasts,
Bodies too big for the minds
That move them. And the sharp,
Short sounds that must be
Signals of wanting, of great feeling.

Alone, I listen for that faint
Whirring as life passes in and out
Of you. I hear sirens
And the bleating of cars parked
Where they will not be left in peace.
Air blows the curtains out and back.

I listen, knowing
You are so far away I must be
Inside you, knowing the night is a great,
Soft, whispering, steady thing
Going on in and around you
And that I am in it.

What Fear Is

Girls with names that mean
Moon or glass or fragrant
Milk-colored flower.

My own figure slipping
From the white palm
Of your upturned heart.

Pale notes
Folded into the grating
Outside your door.

Voices that are not yours
Lining up to touch me
While I pray.

Night

It's almost eleven. There's no reason
To think the man beside me
Can decipher my writing. He watches
The window. A black screen
Interrupted by light. But I do.

The train creeps forward. Stops.
Starts again. The city is long. I can tell
By the way each station is followed
By another. Wall Street.
Bowling Green. It's almost eleven.

The man beside me is asleep now.
Gentle weight against my shoulder.
You're probably cradled in the backseat
Of a taxi, hair wet in that heat,
A few coins making your palm heavy.

Do the houses go past like untouched candies?
Does the fact that nothing's changed
Make you feel like Gulliver
In a toy city, giving the driver directions
To prove to yourself that you're real?

My shoulder thinks the man beside me
Is you, so I don't look. The same way
I don't let my legs sweep the sheets at night
for signs of yours. I am beside you.
Beside myself with you.

In one dream, we're in open air.
Humid night. It's silent. Are all dreams silent?
The train's silent, like an empty house,
And steadfast, as though the only thing
Moving is what surrounds us.

I'm trying to imagine what it feels like
To you just now, tethered to nothing,
Replacing each idea you've guarded
With the thing itself. *Casa. Llave.*
The cat we kept alive

With spilled eggs is gone, I bet.
Across the aisle there's a man
That looks like Pepe, his hands
Two speckled doves gripping a bag
Too small for the bottle it's hiding.

He lunges left, then right,
Holding the bag like a tiny woman
By the waist. Tell me, is it really
That easy for a girl to get
What she wants? I imagine Pepe

In that two-room apartment, Rosy's long hair
Flying as they dance between
The empty spaces. By now you've seen it.
Are there three chairs and three
Chipped bowls? In my night,

There's a woman making a mess
of a Smokey Robinson tune,
And people handing her quarters
So she'll move on to the next car.
When she goes, I feel a little

Like a species of extravagant bird
Has just gone extinct. Maybe your driver
Stops at a light just in time for you to see
An exquisite whore take a swing at vacant air.
Maybe, as the light turns green, you notice

The heel of her shoe has broken off,
And her hands, outstretched for balance,
Flutter like useless wings. It's late. I'm awake
Under fluorescent light. Is it a long ride
To where you're going?

Studio

1.

You breathe against the canvas,
Your eye like a woman
With her legs spread wide,
Bearing down against a future
That is on its way,
That is always almost arriving.

2.

I am that woman knitted into place.
That infant, that smidgen.

I am a skein
Of black hair let loose,
Batted up and back
In a house that grins
Through broken teeth.
An idle form. A nothing.

3.

Strike that. Stroke again
And again. A layer of weather.
Stroke winter. Soon I am new,

Now, am never was.
Disaster in thick gauze.
I bleed from the oldest part of me.

My knees ache with this knowing.

4.

Stretch of my arm
Beyond the edge

Of this solitary, red world.
My brow full, churning.

And reach. The ache—
Like an amputee—

Where my wrist, my
Slender hand ought to be.

5.

I can tell you'll bury me
And start again. Bury me
Thinking of the bodies
You never knew, knew
Briefly. And in long strokes,
I'll disappear.

        Maybe
You'll leave something
Untouched. My sex,
Like a candle.
Lit. Flickering.

Bright

One night as Prince Henry of Portugal lay in bed it was
revealed to him that he would render a great service to our
Lord by the discovery of the said Ethiopias.
　　　　　　　　—Duarte Pachece Pereira, Portuguese Explorer, 1506

The catfish in the kitchen
Drift toward the concave horizon
Of the steel bowl where they sleep,
Drunk now, surely, on cognac,

Honey, green onion. And I hate
The way my teeth rehearse that ceremony.
How my tongue, greedy mollusk,
Flexes in the basin of my mouth.

When the first fair ankles
Waded onto shore on Cape Bianco,
The men balanced above them
Blinked back sweat.

Weeks of salt fish,
Wine, and wind
Like a wife who's glimpsed
Her rival had unsteadied them,

So they weren't sure
At first that what they saw
Wasn't simply the mind
Telling them *Enough*

Or whether it was true.
Lean bodies. Shadows
Incarnate with a grace
Both dark and bright.

As though the world
Were showing off. Black.
Like sable. Like the deep
Center of the darkest fruit,

The first fig. Primordial.
Not sin—not yet—
But satisfaction. Black
As the space between stars,

Distance not fathomed.
Fearsome. Like the restless waves
They'd fought against,
Risk and promise at once.

At first sight
Of those bodies,
Like mine
Or any other—

No: like mine
But intact—why
Did those men,
Asway that entire day,

Seadrunk
On parched land,
Not think:
The Lord is Grand.

Why was that riddle
Not something
They knelt to? Why,
Instead, did they take it as sign

That their want
Should lead them?
The riddle
Doesn't go away.

Even as I push my fork
Into the belly of each
Sleeping fish,
Testing for give, tasting

That distant dream
Of watery flight,
I wonder if you—
Your language of vowels,

Blood that whispers
Back to sails atilt
On some horizon,
Back to men like that—

And I—whose work
Tonight will be
Only to offer—
I wonder if you and I

Have not, perhaps,
Beheld one another—
Flash of teeth, trickle
Of adrenaline—

Elsewhere, and
Before.

The Machinery of Evening

I am looking for my best words.
Willful things
That feint and dart.
If I find them, I will understand
The hunger that stirs us,
That settles like a weight
Pushing us
Into that vivid dark.

Looking with my mouth
Because my eyes will fail.
Because when I find them
I must utter them back
Or they will be lost.
Looking for the words
That do not belong to me
Any more than your body,
Which you offer now.
Any more than these hours,
Which come not to
But for us.

You are looking too
In that language you exhale
Like globes of air
That rise and break
On the surface of what is real.
I love you. These are not
The words any more
Than that hidden skin,
Dark from childhood
In a place too beautiful

To exist, is you.
But I reach for it
And we are closer.

Do you ever wonder
If the answer is what gets said
Again and again
When my body
Houses our two bodies
And we are both
Very briefly
Filled? When we
Open our mouths
And that gladness
Rushes out and around us
And then we sleep, wandering
From screen to screen
In the Cineplex of the mind,
Waking just as a figure
Dressed in gold
Or great folds of green
Is about to speak?

These days, I believe
In everything. That you and I
Are real. That this room,
This simple life
Have gone on
And will go on. These days,
Even the rage
Of unseen neighbors,
Those urgent, animal sounds

That rise to our window
At night, seem to mean.
I don't know why
I want to answer back, want
to give something living back.

In this pause,
This dim hour
Between hours, I want
To be what waits
To be said. I touch you.
Cats throw back their heads
Like furious children.

Dominion over the Beasts of the Earth

> *. . . and whatsoever Adam called every living creature,*
> *that was the name thereof.*
>
> —*Genesis 2:19*

Last night it was Mauricio again,
At the hacienda they say
He and Veronica bought together.
Dark rooms. Floors lain
With exquisite dust. We ran
Back and forth, opening
All the sturdy doors, giddy
As kid goats that have learned
To dance on two hooves.
Breath after breath charging
In and out. Heavy, heavy,
And then weightless, moving
With the prescience of light.

Hazlo que te da
La puta gana. He said it
Over and over. Mauricio—
Enormous Mauricio
With the drunken legs
And hands as large
And white as magnolias—
What would've really happened
If we'd done it that night
In your neighborhood
At the end of the world?
What would we have changed,
Splayed together on that
Rotten mattress
While the buses slept

And the papers curled
Around themselves,
Cradling their news?

I want to speak now
To the ones I've said
Meant nothing,
And I want to call them all
Mauricio.

Mauricio at 13 with skin
Like sunset over the Pacific.
Boy on the cusp, on a bicycle
On the porch my father put up.
Did I stare at my lap,
Wishing myself someone else?
Kathy, with the wild limbs,
A fast girl with bracelets
That made music on her wrists?
And the starlings perched
In rafters—did I invent them?
Tell me, Mauricio, at that age
What does a boy carry with him?

Years later you were tall,
A teacher, a spool
That would not stay wound.
When I burned our letters,
Ordinary moths swarmed my eyes.

I almost even want to speak
To that Mauricio
Who lay awake one whole summer,
Weak with anger, behind me.
Who finally drove off,
Windows obscured by an army
Of striped shirts, but even now
Tries to climb back
Along the frayed thread of dreams.
He stood up to fight once
In a crowded room, insisting
I was his wife. I couldn't laugh
Until I made sure the ring
That married me to the right person
(Two sizes too loose)
Was still on my finger.

Shadow Poem

You know me
But the gauze that fetters the earth
Keeps you from knowing

We were souls together once
Wave after wave of ether
Alive outside of time

I'm still there
Though twice I curled
Into a speck-sized marvel

And waited
In the wet earth of you
Briefly human

You fear everything
And live by a single
Inconstant light

Listening
Hearing nothing
A radio stuck between stations

The second time
I played giddy music
On my blinking heart

Now I watch the dumb machine
Of your body loving
With the loveless wedge of you

That made me

When I want to tell you something
I say it in a voice
The shadow of water

I don't wake you
But the part of you
That's still like me

That rises above your body
When your body
Sinks into itself

The part that doesn't
Belong to you
Knows what it hears

You are not the only one
Alive like that

Prayer

For Yarrow, and all that is bitter.
For the days I rehearse your departure.
For the Yes that is a lie
And the Yes that is not a lie. For You.
For the rivers I will never see. For Yams.
For the way it resembles a woman.
For my mother. For the words
That would not exist without it:
For Yesterday. For not Yet.
For Youth. For Yogurt and the mornings
You feed me. For Yearning.
For what is Yours and not mine.
For the words I repeat in the dark
And the Lord that is always listening.

About Cave Canem

Cave Canem was founded in 1996 by poets Toi Derricotte and Cornelius Eady to promote the artistic development of African American poets. Cave Canem's workshops offer Black poets an opportunity to work together in a welcoming atmosphere and to study with accomplished African American poets and teachers. It has grown into a national community and a home for the rich diversity of Black poetry.

The Cave Canem Poetry Prize is an annual award for the best first collection of poems submitted by an African American poet, selected for publication by an accomplished writer. *The Body's Question* is the 2002 winner of the Cave Canem Poetry Prize, selected by Kevin Young.

The text of this book has been set in Adobe Garamond, drawn by
Robert Slimbach and based on type cut by Claude Garamond in the
sixteenth century.

Book design by Wendy Holdman.
Composition by Stanton Publication Services, Inc., St. Paul, Minnesota.
Manufactured at BookMobile on acid-free 30 percent postconsumer
wastepaper.